SPYING, SURVEILLANCE, AND
PRIVACY IN THE 21st CENTURY

Edward Snowden

Heroic Whistleblower or Traitorous Spy?

Gerry Boehme

Cavendish
Square

New York

Published in 2018 by Cavendish Square Publishing, LLC
243 5th Avenue, Suite 136, New York, NY 10016

Library of Congress Cataloging-in-Publication Data

Names: Boehme, Gerry.
Title: Edward Snowden / Gerry Boehme.
Description: New York : Cavendish Square, 2018. | Series: Spying,
surveillance, and privacy in the 21st-century | Includes index.
Identifiers: ISBN 9781502626738 (library bound) | ISBN 9781502626684 (ebook)
Subjects: LCSH: Snowden, Edward J., 1983- | United States. National
Security Agency/Central Security Service. | Leaks (Disclosure of
information)--United States. | Domestic intelligence--United States.
Classification: LCC JF1525.W45 B64 2018 | DDC 327.1273--dc23

Editorial Director: David McNamara
Editor: Fletcher Doyle
Copy Editor: Nathan Heidelberger
Associate Art Director: Amy Greenan
Designer: Stephanie Flecha
Production Coordinator: Karol Szymczuk
Photo Research: J8 Media

The photographs in this book are used by permission and through the courtesy of:
Cover, Barton Gellman/Getty Images; p. 4 The Guardian/Getty Images; p. 6 Kathy deWitt/Alamy Stock Photo; p. 11
U.S. Navy/File: Pearl Harbor Attack, 7 December 1941 - 80-G-19942.jpg/Wikimedia Commons/Public Domain; p. 13
Marion S. Trikosko/File: Hoover-JEdgar-LOC.jpg/Wikimedia Commons/Public Domain; p. 15 Todd Maisel/NY Daily
News Archive/Getty Images; pp. 21, 80 Bettmann/Getty Images; p. 24 Chip Somodevilla/Getty Images; p. 27 Jason
Merritt/Getty Images; pp. 29, 32 Philippe Lopez /AFP/Getty Images; p. 35 Luke Frazza/AFP/Getty Images; pp. 44,
83 Drew Angerer/Getty Images; p. 47 Mandel Ngan/AFP/Getty Images; p. 50 Mark Wilson/Getty Images; p. 54 AP
Photo/LifeNews via Rossia 24 TV channel; p. 56 Photographer unknown/File: National Security Agency headquarters,
Fort Meade, Maryland.jpg /Wikimedia Commons/Public Domain; p. 65 Marc Piscotty/Getty Images; p. 67 Steffen
Kugler/AFP/Getty Images; p. 69 Trevor Collens/Shutterstock.com; p. 71 AP Photo/Charles Dharapak; p. 76 Larry Ellis/
Express/Getty Images; p. 85 Katherine Frey/The Washington Post/Getty Images; p. 90 Spencer Platt/Getty Images.

Printed in the United States of America

Contents

Edward Snowden created a firestorm when he revealed details about secret US surveillance programs.

CHAPTER 1

Lifting the Veil of Secrecy

On June 5, 2013, a British newspaper, the *Guardian*, published the first in a series of articles that shocked the world. Using **classified** documents stolen from inside the deepest levels of the US government, author Glenn Greenwald revealed details about secret electronic **espionage** activities conducted by the National Security Agency (**NSA**) that had been hidden even from the top levels of American leadership. The documents revealed a vast and complex system of domestic and international **surveillance**, including the secret collection of telephone and internet communications from people all over the globe.

The NSA surveillance programs spied on US citizens and noncitizens alike and included everyone from ordinary people to the highest government officials. Everything was fair game—telephone conversations, texts, email messages, web browsing, and live streams from laptop and mobile phone cameras. The evidence proved that the NSA had either been given access to or had **hacked** into the internal records of many of the world's largest **telecommunications**

International

Secret back door enables NSA to spy on messages of US citizens

New Snowden revelation on emails and phone calls

Law-abiding Americans 'spied on without warrant'

James Ball and Spencer Ackerman

The National Security Agency has a secret back door into its databases under a legal authority enabling it to search for US citizens' email and phone calls without a warrant, according to a top secret document passed to the Guardian by Edward Snowden.

The previously undisclosed rule change allows NSA operatives to hunt for individual Americans' communications using their name or other identifying information. Senator Ron Wyden told the Guardian the authority enables "warrantless searches for the phone calls or emails of law-abiding Americans".

The authority, approved in 2011, appears to contrast with repeated assurances from Barack Obama and senior intelligence officials to both Congress and the American public that the privacy of US citizens is protected from the NSA's dragnet surveillance programs.

You can't that hand $77m-a-y Winfrey t

Adam Gabbatt New Y

The world learned of US electronic spying when the *Guardian* printed articles based on Snowden's files.

companies and even the private mobile phone conversations of international leaders.

Over the next few days, additional articles appeared in the *Guardian* as well as other publications, including the *Washington Post* and the *New York Times*. Incredibly, all the secret documents and files came from a single, anonymous **whistleblower**, a person who had worked in security for the US government and obviously had access to the deepest levels of highly sensitive data. Just four days later, on June 9, the source revealed his identity to the world.

Meet Edward Snowden

Edward Snowden, a mild-mannered twenty-nine-year-old **contractor** who worked for the NSA, had just become one of the most famous and controversial figures in recent history. As a systems administrator responsible for maintaining and repairing networks, Snowden managed to access a broad range of classified NSA programs and files. For reasons he would soon explain, Snowden decided to collect, steal, and release thousands of top-secret documents that cast a bright light on the NSA's most hidden surveillance practices.

Who exactly was this Edward Snowden? And what motivated him to secretly gather and then release tremendously sensitive material that pulled back the curtain on the innermost workings of United States's national security operations?

Edward Snowden was born June 21, 1983, in Elizabeth City, North Carolina. Both of his parents worked for the government, and his older sister later joined them. Snowden's father, Lonnie, served as an officer in the Coast Guard; his mother, Wendy, clerked for a federal court; his sister, Jessica, worked in research for the Federal Judicial Center. When Edward was young, the family moved to Crofton, Maryland, a suburb of Washington, DC, an area where many people work for the US government. Edward thought he would as well.

People who knew Snowden as a child describe him as nice, shy, quiet, and thin. He joined the boy scouts and is remembered as a "computer nerd." When his parents divorced after he left high school, Snowden went to live with his mother in a small condo while his father moved to Allentown, Pennsylvania.

Many details of Snowden's life are sketchy at best. He is reported to be a high school dropout but also a brilliant student. According to some reports, he contracted mononucleosis in tenth grade and missed most of the year. Rather than starting over to make up the time, Snowden took an exam to get his high school diploma and then entered Anne Arundel Community College at the age of sixteen. The college offered courses in **cyberspace** security for people who were interested in working for the NSA. While Snowden did not take those classes, he knew many students who did.

During that time, Snowden showed strong interest in technology, computer games, social media, online chat rooms, and fantasy comics. He especially liked **manga**, a kind of Japanese comic, and video games that featured fighting and demonstrated a clear sense of right and wrong. He and some friends eventually moved into an apartment in Maryland near Fort Meade, home of the NSA.

When the United States invaded Iraq in 2003, Snowden decided to enlist in the US Army, hoping to join the elite special forces. He was motivated in part by traditional patriotism and support for the government, but he also wanted to help free the people of Iraq from Saddam Hussein's dictatorship. Snowden quickly became disenchanted with the US military, however, later saying that he heard more talk about killing than about helping the Iraqi people.

Snowden's military career was short-lived. He reportedly broke both of his legs in a training accident and was soon discharged. After leaving the army, Snowden searched for a job with the area's largest employer—the NSA—and began working there in 2005. He started as a security guard, but people soon noticed his talent in technology and he quickly advanced to a position at the Central Intelligence Agency (**CIA**). It wasn't long before Snowden was earning a six-figure salary.

The Power of Information

Working with the NSA and the CIA gave Snowden his first opportunity to experience how the United States conducted its secret surveillance and espionage operations. He saw how information could be collected and analyzed to protect America's citizens and defeat its enemies. On the other hand, he also witnessed how that same information could be used in ways that the law and the US Constitution never intended.

English author, politician, and philosopher Sir Francis Bacon is often credited for coining the phrase "information is power" late in the sixteenth century. Good information contributes to knowledge and helps people make smart decisions. By controlling access to information, however, powerful people can influence the thoughts and actions of others. Author Tom Clancy once said, "The control of information is something the elite always does, particularly in a despotic form of government … If you can control information, you can control people."

The earliest governments realized that they needed to establish ways to collect and analyze information. Just as important, doing that in secret could provide advantages over foreign enemies and even opponents at home.

Spies and Surveillance

The history of espionage and secret spying goes back to the beginnings of recorded history. The Egyptians used a form of secret surveillance to gather information about their enemies, and ancient Chinese documents state that all war is based on deception and intelligence gathering. Medieval European powers like England and France employed networks to gather secret intelligence, and the American Revolution immortalized the names of spies like Nathan Hale and Benedict Arnold.

After America gained its independence from Great Britain, the Founding Fathers debated the relative merits of letting citizens know everything versus the need for secrecy. While they championed the goal of governmental transparency and supported the idea of an informed citizenry, the Constitutional Convention also met and discussed some issues in private, and the Constitution authorized Congress to keep some of its work hidden from its citizens.

Even the new government's structure spoke to the balance between keeping everyone informed versus limiting certain facts to those responsible for managing the country's affairs. In the American system, sometimes called a "representative democracy," elected officials sometimes make decisions that are based on information hidden from the general population.

The Espionage Act

By the start of World War I (1914–1918), all the world's great powers except the United States had built extensive espionage and spy networks. While the United States stayed out of the war at first, it recognized the need to take a greater role internationally as well as to protect the country against foreign agents. Shortly before the country entered World War I, the US Congress passed the Espionage Act of 1917. The legislation was primarily intended to limit information about the country's intentions to enter World War I, which had been raging in Europe for almost three years, as well as to suppress dissent from Americans who opposed participation in the war. The Espionage Act made it a crime to "furnish, transmit or communicate" US intelligence material to a foreign government. However, some language in the act was vague, including whether it applied to journalists who published articles critical of the war.

Pearl Harbor and the NSA

On December 7, 1941, Japan launched a successful surprise attack on the United States Navy at its main Pacific base at Pearl Harbor, Hawaii. The Japanese had managed to assemble a large naval force and sail it across the Pacific Ocean while remaining completely undetected. Their success indicated a massive failure of American intelligence operations. In response, the United States committed to building a stronger and more effective secret intelligence and espionage operation. Decisions made back then helped to shape the national security organizations we see today.

A plan for a new security organization was drafted and presented to President Franklin D. Roosevelt on November 18, 1944. It envisioned an independent agency directly responsible to the president and authorized to carry out espionage and counterespionage activities, "subversive operations abroad," and "such other functions and duties

The surprise Japanese attack on Pearl Harbor exposed weaknesses in US intelligence capabilities.

related to intelligence." Even during that time some people viewed the plan with suspicion and even fear. Walter Trohan, a well-respected newspaper reporter back then, called the proposal a "super spy system" that would "pry into the lives of citizens at home."

During World War II, systems for espionage and intelligence grew considerably larger and more sophisticated in countries all over the world. The programs continued to expand in the postwar years during what became known as the Cold War, a time when tensions escalated between the United States and its allies against the forces of communism and the Union of Soviet Socialist Republics (USSR, or Soviet Union). In the United States, the 1947 National Security Act created the CIA to coordinate intelligence gathering. In 1952, the NSA was established to set policy and concentrate on electronic communication. Meanwhile, the USSR developed its own infrastructure to support surveillance and espionage under its Committee for State Security (the KGB), which also acted as a secret police force.

As national systems of espionage and data collection continued to grow, governments around the world began to believe that their records and even the methods of collection themselves needed to be hidden from enemies, allies, and even their own citizens. America was no exception. In 1951, President Harry S. Truman directed all federal agencies to classify records as secret in the name of "national security."

As the veil of secrecy grew, the US government began to collect and use secret information in new ways that made some people increasingly uncomfortable. For example, in 1938 President Roosevelt allowed the Federal Bureau of Investigation (**FBI**) to secretly investigate the beliefs and noncriminal activities of ordinary Americans and to conceal

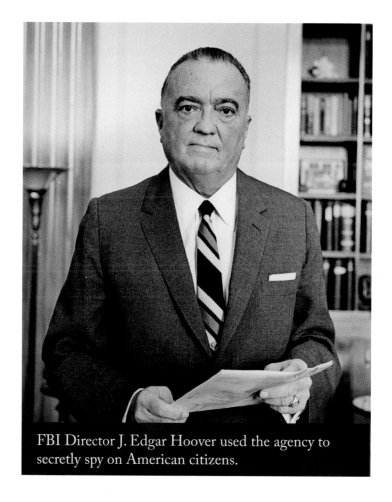
FBI Director J. Edgar Hoover used the agency to secretly spy on American citizens.

those efforts from Congress and the American public. While some defended these programs as necessary to identify threats against the country, others argued that the government was beginning to violate the rights and privacy of the very citizens it was sworn to protect.

Others were even more fearful that government officials would begin to use these powerful tools for their own selfish purposes. In one glaring case during the 1970s, President Richard Nixon ordered the NSA to tap the phones of Americans he did not like, including critics of his administration and especially activists who opposed the Vietnam War.

One way to help protect the rights of American citizens was to ensure that American security agencies could not simply decide on their own to investigate American citizens. Intelligence and law enforcement agencies were required to go to court and convince a judge that there were good reasons to suspect and investigate someone for illegal activity. If the judge agreed, the court could grant a warrant to authorize surveillance. This arrangement helped to preserve the balance of power between the agencies tasked with investigating crime and courts responsible for determining guilt or innocence.

Twin Towers and Terrorism

On September 11, 2001, the situation changed for everyone.

When the Islamic terrorist organization al-Qaeda attacked the World Trade Center in New York City and the Pentagon outside of Washington, DC, Americans were forced to come to grips with a new reality. Secret terrorist organizations not affiliated with any specific country could now plan and execute devastating attacks anywhere on the planet. This new world required a total reexamination of how to best confront this dangerous threat.

Regardless of whether they did not gather enough information or were unable to analyze it properly, American intelligence organizations had clearly failed to discover and prevent the 9/11 attacks. In response, the government authorized the NSA to expand its efforts to gather vast amounts of electronic data to identify and stop future terrorist assaults.

The government directed the NSA to expand its surveillance programs after the 9/11 terrorist attacks.

The PATRIOT Act

In late October 2001, less than two months after 9/11, President George W. Bush asked Congress to pass the USA PATRIOT Act (officially known as the Uniting and Strengthening America by Providing Appropriate Tools Required to Intercept and Obstruct Terrorism Act of

2001). The PATRIOT Act greatly expanded the ability of the US Department of Justice (DOJ), the NSA, and other federal agencies to secretly collect and store electronic communications both in the United States and abroad. It also allowed agencies to share information and coordinate strategies against terrorism.

The NSA began to develop new programs to collect information from many different sources, including telecom and internet companies. The NSA soon realized that, since so much data could be collected, it was difficult to predict in advance what would be useful or how to analyze it once it arrived. The NSA decided to first collect everything it could, then develop the means to search the data afterward to find patterns of suspicious activity.

While everyone agreed that it was important to catch the 9/11 terrorists and work to prevent more attacks, some still feared that personal privacy rights could be trampled if an emotional response led American security agencies to expand electronic surveillance without adequate safeguards. Their concerns were soon confirmed.

In December 2005, the *New York Times* reported that, shortly after 9/11, President Bush secretly authorized the National Security Agency to eavesdrop on Americans and others inside the United States without first obtaining the court-approved warrants that were legally required for domestic spying. Most people in government did not know about the program until the *Times* broke the story. Additionally, the NSA had previously told government officials, the *Times*, and telecommunications providers that the program was legal.

Electronic Surveillance and You

Technology has changed the way people communicate. Mobile devices and the internet help people to stay connected twenty-four hours a day, seven days a week. Millions upon millions of text messages, phone calls, photos, and videos flow across the world's electronic systems every minute.

While advances in communication and information technology certainly have their advantages, they also pose great risks to personal privacy. In reality, no modern communications are truly private. All messages and requests for information are electronically transmitted through a wide variety of telecommunications connections. Many can be intercepted, stored, and searched by a multitude of companies and organizations, including governments.

While leakers like Edward Snowden have pointed out how much information governments collect on their citizens, the same can be said for schools and businesses as well. Social sites like Facebook track every action and every response. Advertisers collect information that they use to target each person with ads designed to make you spend more on their products. Colleges and employers now have the ability to view online profiles and behavior to decide whether to accept someone as a student or offer them a job.

How comfortable are you that private companies as well as the government may be storing information about where you go, what you do, whom you talk to, and what you think? Do you believe that we should give up some privacy in order to be safer? The issues raised by Edward Snowden will continue to increase in importance as electronic systems continue to advance.

The Role of Whistleblowers

The conflict pitting the government's need to keep sensitive information secret in order to keep the country safe against the citizens' desire to hold the government accountable for wrongdoings such as illegal searches was nothing new. In fact, long before Snowden's **leak**, people within the security agencies themselves had raised concerns about the level of surveillance and abuses of government power they witnessed. Some even decided to become whistleblowers and reveal details about programs that they thought broke the law.

In 1971, a government advisor named Daniel Ellsberg (see sidebar on page 20) leaked a series of documents known as the Pentagon Papers to the *New York Times* that exposed a history of government lies and deceptions about the Vietnam War. In 2006, the *Baltimore Sun* published articles about waste and illegal surveillance based on information supplied by Thomas Drake, an NSA employee. In 2010, a US Army private, Chelsea Manning, posted millions of pages of classified diplomatic cables and government documents about the wars in Iraq and Afghanistan to **WikiLeaks**.

Each case sparked debates within the government organizations themselves, as well as among the American people, about whether secretly intercepting, storing, and analyzing information violated the public's right to know and their expectations of privacy. The cases also displayed the government's power to attack the leakers on both professional and personal levels, including charging them with serious crimes such as violations of the Espionage Act and even treason.

In his book *The War On Leakers*, author Lloyd Gardner writes, "There has always been a campaign against leakers and ... a desire to put leakers and protesters in the same bin as foreign spies and cast enforcement actions in terms of a 'balance' between liberty and security."

Game Changer

As he became more deeply involved with the operations of the NSA, Edward Snowden decided to make his own mark in this shadowy world of secret surveillance and questions of privacy.

In 2007, when he was twenty-four, the CIA transferred Snowden overseas as a "telecommunications information systems officer," where he worked in cyber security for US diplomats stationed in Geneva, Switzerland. Up until that time, Snowden still largely supported government policies. He had even **blogged** against previous leakers, writing that the government kept secrets "for a reason" and that the leakers were "violating national security." Snowden's move to Geneva and his work with the NSA while stationed there began to change his views on America's espionage activities.

During his time in Geneva, Snowden discovered that CIA agents had blackmailed a Swiss banker, threatening to reveal harmful personal information, to force him to reveal secret financial data. He heard agents discuss US policy in Iraq and Afghanistan, often criticizing government decision making and its use of information. Snowden also witnessed what he believed to be human rights abuses, including the torture of suspected militants and electronic eavesdropping without a court order. He began to feel conflicted about what the NSA did and the role that he played.

"Much of what I saw in Geneva really disillusioned me about how my government functions and what its impact is in the world," Snowden told the *Guardian*. "I realized that I was part of something that was doing far more harm than good."

Daniel Ellsberg and the Pentagon Papers

After serving as a US marine in the 1950s, Daniel Ellsberg worked with the US government as an advisor on military strategy. His responsibilities included studying America's growing involvement in the war in Vietnam. In 1965, he moved to Vietnam to observe the situation firsthand.

Ellsberg originally supported the government's approach. During his two years in Vietnam, however, he saw a difference between what US officials told the public versus what they said in private about their plans and the chances for success.

After returning to the United States, Ellsberg worked on a top-secret report about America's Vietnam policy from 1945 through 1968. Ellsberg's report showed that several previous administrations had publicly claimed they were working to end the war while they privately took action to expand it. Ellsberg called the report "evidence of a quarter century of aggression, broken treaties, deceptions, stolen elections, lies and murder."

Working with officials in President Richard Nixon's administration, Ellsberg grew increasingly frustrated with their insistence on continuing down the same path. Ellsberg decided to end what he saw as his complicity with the Vietnam War and start working to bring about the war's end.

"My thought was to expose and subvert the very process of presidential lying about war policy," Ellsberg later remembered. Knowing that his actions could come at great personal risk, Ellsberg recalled, "Their example put the

Daniel Ellsberg (*left*) released the "Pentagon Papers," secret documents about the Vietnam War.

question in my head: What could I do to help shorten this war, now that I'm prepared to go to prison for it?"

Ellsberg copied the report's more than seven thousand pages. After offering it to several congressmen, who refused to make the documents public, he leaked it to the *New York Times* and other newspapers in 1971. The release of what came to be known as "The Pentagon Papers" inflamed opposition to the unpopular war.

For leaking the Pentagon Papers, Ellsberg was charged with theft, conspiracy, and violations of the Espionage Act. The case was dismissed after it became known that the Nixon administration had tried to discredit Ellsberg by illegally wiretapping his phone and entering his psychiatrist's office to steal personal information.

Many people called Ellsberg a traitor. Most now consider him to be a hero who risked his career and his freedom to expose government deception.

Shoot the Messenger

During that period, Snowden also noticed vulnerabilities in a CIA program. To prove it, he successfully hacked into the system with his supervisor's approval. Snowden hoped that his actions would spur the agency to improve the software's security. Instead, his superiors were more upset that weaknesses in the system had been publicly exposed and reprimanded him for breaking into it. Their response may have taught Snowden that if you work within the system to make changes, you will be punished for it.

In February 2009, Snowden resigned from the CIA and went to work as a contractor for Dell, a computer and technology company. He was assigned to an NSA office near Tokyo. His job was to advise American and Japanese military officials on how to protect their systems from Chinese hacker attacks. While in Japan, Snowden again witnessed things that disturbed him, including drone attacks and targeted killings. He also learned that the NSA could now track everyone in a city through their smartphones and other electronic devices.

For Edward Snowden, the time had come for him to decide whether to continue to work within the US security establishment, or to tell others outside the government what was really happening. In his book *The Snowden Files*, author Luke Harden writes, "Japan marks a turning point. It is the period when Snowden goes from disillusioned technician to proto-whistleblower."

In March 2012, Snowden applied for a transfer to the NSA regional office near Honolulu in Hawaii. It specialized in surveillance of China. After a short time, he moved from Dell to Booz Allen Hamilton, another NSA contractor. Snowden decided to steal top-secret files containing information about the NSA's illegal surveillance of US citizens and to leak them to reputable independent journalists brave enough to present the facts to the public.

In December 2012, Snowden anonymously contacted Glenn Greenwald, a columnist for the *Guardian* as well as a civil liberties attorney and a known critic of the US government. He also reached out to Laura Poitras, an independent **documentary** filmmaker. It took months to set up **encrypted** communications and for Snowden to prove they could trust him. On May 20, 2013, Snowden left Hawaii and flew to Hong Kong, where he first met Greenwald and Poitras on June 1. He gave them access to all of his stolen files within a short time frame.

The *Guardian* published its first article about the secret NSA espionage on June 5. Within just a few days, governments and citizens all over the world became involved in an intense debate about whether Edward Snowden was a courageous whistleblower or a cowardly traitor.

Glenn Greenwald wrote the first stories based on Edward Snowden's revelations.

CHAPTER 2

Compelled
to Act

In the fall of 2005, writer and lawyer Glenn Greenwald decided to create a political blog. "My principal motive," he wrote afterward, "was that I was becoming increasingly alarmed by the radical and extremist theories of power the US government had adopted in the wake of 9/11, and I hoped that writing about such issues might allow me to make a broader impact than I could in my then-career as a constitutional and civil rights lawyer." He later admitted, "I had little idea at the time how much this decision would eventually change my life."

Only weeks after Greenwald started his blog, the *New York Times* reported that the Bush administration had secretly ordered the NSA to monitor electronic communications of Americans without asking for court warrants that were required by law. The surveillance had been going on for four years since 9/11.

Government officials defended the program by claiming that the threat of terrorism gave the president almost unlimited authority to keep the nation safe, even if it meant breaking the law. According to Greenwald, "the ensuing debate entailed complex questions of constitutional law and statutory interpretation," and his experience as a lawyer qualified him to write about the issue. Greenwald spent the next two years covering the surveillance program on his blog and in a book he wrote in 2006.

An Anonymous Contact

Greenwald soon became well known for covering stories dealing with government security practices and what he felt were violations of the law and personal privacy. In 2007, Greenwald started writing for the internet magazine *Salon*. He then moved to the British-based newspaper the *Guardian* in 2012 when it opened an office in New York City.

On December 12, 2012, Greenwald received an email from someone who called himself "Cincinnatus." The unusual name referred to a fifth-century-BCE Roman farmer who, after being appointed to defend Rome and then defeating its enemies, immediately gave up his power and returned to farming. Since that time, the name Cincinnatus has symbolized using political power to benefit citizens, but also relinquishing that power for the common good.

This modern-day Cincinnatus claimed that he had an important story to tell about the government. First, however, he insisted that Greenwald use encryption for all his emails to make sure that they remained completely confidential and secure from outside examination. Greenwald was initially suspicious; many other people had contacted him with what they said were "big" stories that later turned out to hold little value. Greenwald was also busy with other projects, and he thought that encrypting his emails would be very complex and time consuming.

Greenwald delayed responding for several weeks, but he kept wondering whether Cincinnatus did indeed have something significant to offer. It wasn't until he heard from Laura Poitras, a controversial documentary filmmaker whom he knew and respected, that Greenwald took Cincinnatus seriously.

Poitras told Greenwald that the same anonymous person had contacted her. After agreeing to encrypt her systems, she received a series of emails that she showed to Greenwald. He found them, in his words, "riveting." The source said he had stolen detailed, classified documents that proved the US government was using advanced electronic systems to secretly spy on people all over the world, including Americans. Teaming with Poitras, Greenwald decided to find out what this anonymous person could reveal about the US secret surveillance program.

Director Laura Poitras (*center*) won the Academy Award (Best Documentary Feature) for *Citizenfour*.

Meeting in Hong Kong

The source now used the code name "Verax," which is Latin for "truth teller." Two other men had used the name Verax to air dissenting views against their government. Clement Walker, a seventeenth-century critic of the English Parliament, had been imprisoned and later died in the Tower of London. In the late 1880s, an Englishman named Henry Dunckley wrote a series of articles supporting the rights of the lower classes.

Verax asked Greenwald and Poitras to meet with him in person. In the meantime, he provided a set of documents for them to study, including more secret NSA files, and more reasons why he decided to leak them. Verax also revealed an additional important detail: his true identity. Edward Snowden, former NSA advisor and former CIA field officer, had stepped forward from the shadows.

On June 1, 2013, Greenwald and Poitras flew to Hong Kong to talk with Snowden. They had never seen him in person, so Snowden held a Rubik's Cube so they could identify him when they met in a hotel lobby. In the days that followed, Snowden shared with them more than 1.7 million files from US intelligence, as well as thousands of files that Great Britain and other countries had shared with the United States. In the book that he wrote about the Snowden affair, *No Place to Hide*, Greenwald calls the documents "powerful and shocking."

Collect Everything About Everything

The sheer scale of the surveillance was breathtaking. Snowden revealed a number of classified US surveillance programs, including a massive internet data-mining system. The NSA had secretly tapped into undersea fiber-optic cables around

Edward Snowden's revelations generated protests against the collection of data from major companies.

the globe that carried most of the world's communications. The process was electronic and automated; the data was collected and stored for later use.

The NSA information included something called **metadata**, which can be described as "data about data." For example, metadata for your telephone calls might include the number you called from and its owner (you), all the numbers you called and who owned them, the duration of each call, the time and date you called, and both your location and the recipient's. These huge amounts of information then could be searched based on a specific set of criteria. For example, keyword searches could include terms like "terrorism," "Islam," or anything else the NSA wanted.

Snowden's documents alleged that many internet companies provided information to the NSA, including Google, Microsoft, Yahoo!, Skype, AOL, YouTube, and Facebook. Sometimes the companies were compelled secretly to cooperate by orders from US courts.

The NSA's surveillance capabilities seemed boundless. All electronic activity could be harvested and stored—voice calls, emails, texts, online chats, gaming, web browsing, app downloads, streaming video, and online shopping. Audio from telephone calls could be played back five years after they occurred. Smartphones could be used to track movements and hear conversations even if they were turned off. Cameras on phones, computers, and even smart TVs could be activated to spy on unsuspecting people in their most private moments.

The NSA even inserted secret back doors into encryption software, such as that used by online banks. The back doors allowed the NSA to access confidential transactions. By breaking the encryption security, the back doors may have also weakened the systems by making it easier for others to also hack in.

Citizens Included

American citizens were not supposed to be targeted in this program. In fact, the NSA's charter authorized it to collect information only about people outside of the United States. Regardless, it appeared that sensitive conversations, photos, and videos of Americans were included, intentionally or not. After being stored, any person's information could be scooped up later and read "accidentally" by any low-level analyst, with no need to get court or supervisor approval.

While giving itself unprecedented surveillance powers, the US intelligence community also concealed the truth about the program. The US Senate had called NSA personnel to testify under oath about their surveillance activities, but some had lied and said they did not spy on Americans.

And, in what might be considered an ironic twist, the NSA also supplied data to the security organizations of US allies who were banned by their own laws from gathering it themselves.

An operation of this size required tens of thousands of employees, and even more contractors, to make it work. Organizations like the FBI, CIA, DHS (Department of Homeland Security), and the DIA (Defense Intelligence Agency) were all involved, as well as private contractors from perhaps thousands of different companies. Nearly 1.5 million people may have taken part, many of whom had access to private information.

In short, Snowden said, the US government had spent hundreds of millions of dollars to build the most sophisticated surveillance network ever imagined, all in secret, and much of it arguably against the law. Furthermore, the system of checks and balances that had supposedly been built into the program by the NSA itself, as well as by Congress and the US courts, did not seem to be working.

Why Snowden?

So why did Snowden do it? Others had seen the same NSA programs and systems but did not come forward. Why did he? What made him react so strongly that he would risk his

Edward Snowden got support in Hong Kong right after the first *Guardian* articles were published.

freedom and give up a comfortable life in order to expose the entire NSA surveillance program?

Snowden knew that some of his coworkers were uncomfortable with the extent of the NSA's actions but still felt they were legal. Others may have questioned their lawfulness, but they still thought the surveillance was necessary to prevent attacks and protect Americans. Perhaps they believed that the government would not take any action that jeopardized the best interests of the American people. Still others may have agreed with Snowden, but they may also have been afraid of being fired, sued, or even arrested if they violated their promises of confidentiality, made when hired, to go public with their concerns.

Edward Snowden clearly thought differently. He did more than just leak the documents; on June 9, the *Guardian* revealed Snowden's identity at his request. At the time, Snowden explained that he did not want any of his colleagues to fall under suspicion or be accused of being the source. He also felt that the NSA would eventually figure out he was the leaker and track him down. And, perhaps most important, Snowden said, "I have no intention of hiding who I am because I know I have done nothing wrong."

In *No Place to Hide*, Glenn Greenwald says that Snowden repeatedly emphasized that his goal was not to destroy the NSA's capability to eliminate privacy. Snowden told Greenwald:

It's not my role to make that choice. I don't intend to destroy these systems, but to allow the public to decide whether they should go on.

Snowden's revelations sparked a furious worldwide debate. Some called him a coward and a traitor. Others quickly rose to his defense, citing many reasons why Snowden was justified in his actions.

Secrecy and the Law

Some people claim that the NSA activity was legal, legitimized under the secret rulings of the Foreign Intelligence Surveillance Court (FISC), a US federal court established and authorized under the Foreign Intelligence Surveillance Act of 1978 (FISA). The court's main purpose is to decide whether to grant certain types of government requests, such as wiretapping and other types of surveillance, to target suspected terrorists and spies operating in the United States.

Opponents argue that most FISC requests, deliberations, and decisions are conducted in secret, and that the court only considers the government's position. They also disagree with the NSA's claims of legality. They argue that the court's original mission was incorrectly expanded and that it was interpreting requests for surveillance too broadly, harming rights to privacy and due process. Perhaps the laws could have been changed to address the new threats posed by terrorism, but the NSA should have followed the laws that existed. These critics feel that NSA policies need to be publicly considered, debated, and decided.

Writing about Snowden and his fight against the secrecy of NSA activities, William E. Scheuerman, a professor of political science at Indiana University, says that "Publicity is fundamental to the rule of law and constitutional government, whereas secret law tends to be corrosive, as it risks unduly veiling government action from individual and collective scrutiny."

Pure Motives

While some accuse Snowden of acting out of selfishness or greed, or putting others in danger, his defenders believe otherwise.

There have been many examples of US citizens enriching themselves by spying for foreign governments. CIA analyst Aldrich Ames was convicted of espionage in 1994 after working directly for the KGB and selling secrets in return for $4.6 million. In 2001, former FBI agent Robert Hanssen was convicted of selling sensitive information to the Soviet Union and then Russia over a period of more than twenty years in return for $1.4 million.

There is no evidence that Snowden leaked NSA documents for his own financial gain. In fact, he left a high-paying job, his home, and his girlfriend in order to meet with journalists and reveal the NSA's surveillance programs. He currently lives modestly at best in Russia, reportedly with girlfriend Lindsay Mills, and shows no signs of amassing any wealth.

Spies like Ames and Hanssen worked directly with hostile foreign governments, and they supplied specific information that named American agents and identified operations that put US citizens at risk.

Former senior CIA officer Aldrich Ames went to prison for selling information to the Soviet Union.

Snowden, on the other hand, claims that he has not released any information directly to any foreign government. He says he refused requests from Russia to access his documents, which he protected with advanced encryption techniques, one of his specialties. He was determined to prevent any foreign intelligence service from gaining access, and he did not want to damage intelligence operations abroad.

No Direct Public Release

Snowden did not go directly to the public with his leaks; he only released the documents to journalists he trusted to look carefully at the content and not reveal anything that would harm national security. Furthermore, Snowden insisted on strict conditions before he provided his material to Greenwald, Poitras, and other journalists.

Snowden also says he only provided documents about the capabilities and extent of NSA systems, not the actual information that they collected. He did not download information about rosters of employees, assignments, or locations, and he did not provide any information on people working for the NSA or any other agency for fear of exposing them to danger.

Following His Conscience

According to Snowden, once he began to feel that the NSA surveillance was wrong, he felt he had a moral responsibility to follow his conscience and to act. Snowden quoted the **Nuremberg Tribunal's** rebuke to Nazi war criminals who claimed that they were just following orders when they committed their ghastly crimes against humanity during

World War II. The tribunal ruled that "individuals have international duties which transcend the national obligations of obedience."

Like many other Americans, Snowden heard about earlier situations in which government agencies abused their power to unjustly target Americans and violate their rights. Many had occurred with or without the approval of others in the government, including the president.

In the 1950s, the FBI used a **counterintelligence** program known as COINTELPRO to disrupt the activities of the Communist Party of the United States. The FBI expanded the program in the 1960s to include a number of other domestic groups. It ended in 1971, and even the FBI's official website admits that, "COINTELPRO was later rightfully criticized by Congress and the American people for abridging first amendment rights and for other reasons." The FBI also spied on civil rights leader Martin Luther King Jr. in an attempt to uncover embarrassing information that would hurt his cause.

The CIA once enlisted Mafia leaders to try to assassinate Cuban leader Fidel Castro after his forces took over the country. The CIA also worked with the Atomic Energy Commission to secretly conduct experiments on American citizens to test the effects of radiation and drugs on human behavior and health.

In all these cases and many others, the government classified documents that may have been embarrassing or that would have exposed illegal activity in order to hide them from public examination and scrutiny.

Danger from Technology

Snowden's expertise centered on advanced technology, and perhaps that influenced his decision as much as anything else he experienced. Snowden understood better than most the ramifications of the NSA's surveillance program, and how it could become even more dangerous as technology continued to advance.

Snowden told Greenwald that he was especially concerned with preserving privacy on the internet. Snowden had used the internet as a teenager to explore ideas and speak with people in faraway places and from different backgrounds, and he wanted to preserve that right for others. "That works only if we're able to be private and anonymous, to make mistakes without them following us," Snowden said. "I worry that mine was the last generation to enjoy that freedom."

Snowden hoped that by revealing the NSA's practices, he could motivate technology companies to resist government efforts to collect their records as well as develop better security and encryption programs to protect individual privacy.

As the debate over Snowden raged on, the conversation extended beyond specific NSA surveillance programs to include even broader issues.

Personal Privacy and the Constitution

To many people, it was clear that the NSA's program violated a person's right to privacy. *New York Times* columnist David Brooks stressed the importance of personal privacy when he wrote about another subject related to safety and security, the increased use of body-mounted cameras by police:

> There has to be an interior zone within each person that other people don't see. There has to be a zone where half-formed thoughts and delicate emotions can grow and evolve, without being exposed to the

harsh glare of public judgment … There has to be a private space where you can share your doubts and secrets and expose your weaknesses with the expectation that you will still be loved and forgiven and supported.

Beyond simply the need for privacy, many Snowden supporters argue that the NSA programs violated specific articles of the US Constitution and international law. William Scheuerman writes that the NSA surveillance violated the Fourth and Fifth Amendments to the US Constitution (which prohibit unreasonable seizures and guarantee basic due process), as well as Article 12 of the Universal Declaration of Human Rights (which protects against arbitrary interference with a person's privacy) and international treaties that ban legally unchecked state surveillance. The Fourth Amendment reads in part:

> The right of the people to be secure in their persons, houses, papers, and effects, against unreasonable searches and seizures, shall not be violated, and no warrants shall issue, but upon probable cause, supported by oath or affirmation, and particularly describing the place to be searched, and the persons or things to be seized.

While technology may have changed a great deal since the Constitution was written, Snowden's supporters believe that the very specific language of the Fourth Amendment clearly forbids programs like the NSA's secret surveillance. A person's home, communications, and possessions cannot be indiscriminately collected without a warrant and clear evidence of potential wrongdoing.

Civil Disobedience

William Scheuerman also believes that Snowden's actions fall under the definition of civil disobedience. He writes that Snowden followed the examples of famous leaders like Martin Luther King and Mahatma Gandhi, who broke the law in nonviolent ways to expose and correct illegal or unjust government policies and practices. In his book *The Snowden Reader*, Scheuerman includes an entry on civil disobedience, writing:

> Unfortunately, the hoopla [around Snowden] has obscured a more vital part of the story, namely the moral and political seriousness with which Snowden acted to make covert NSA surveillance public knowledge. As we know now, and as Snowden anticipated, his decision came at a huge personal cost … Snowden's public declarations … show that [he] thought long and hard about the question of when and how citizens of a liberal democratic state are morally and politically obliged to violate the law.

While some claim that a civil disobedience defense requires that Snowden return to the United States and accept punishment, his defenders answer that the punishment would be neither fair nor just. It would be difficult for Snowden to mount a public defense because the documents he released remain classified and could not be used. They also say he has already accepted punishment by voluntarily giving up a good life in the United States and living under harsh conditions in Russia.

Misapplication of the Espionage Act

The government has used the Espionage Act to target many leakers, including Snowden. The Espionage Act dates back to 1917 and centers on a person's exposure of classified information. However, many legal experts claim that the Espionage Act does not apply to Snowden, since it states that the guilty person has to aid an enemy of the United States. Snowden did not directly reveal any information to a foreign country or enemy. He released it to newspapers, which in turn made the choice to inform the public.

Some countries have what is called an "official secrets act," which places emphasis on the material itself rather than the behavior of the person who leaks it. If the government declares a piece of information to be an official secret, then someone can be prosecuted for simply revealing that secret.

The United States has never enacted an official secrets act, largely because the Constitution defends individual rights over the government's choice to hide information. That makes it difficult for the government to declare any piece of information an "official secret" and then use that definition to hide information from the press and the public.

Some people believe that the government uses the Espionage Act to get around the First Amendment, which guarantees freedom of the press, when the government wants to keep certain information hidden. By its name, the Espionage Act also labels the accused person as disloyal, if not guilty of outright treason. That connotation, combined with potentially significant legal penalties and expenses,

Reining In the NSA

Edward Snowden's revelations about the NSA surveillance programs even shocked Republican congressman James Sensenbrenner, who had coauthored the PATRIOT Act. He felt betrayed by the NSA's actions, stating, "I can say that if Congress knew what the NSA had in mind in the future immediately after 9/11, the PATRIOT Act never would have passed, and I never would have supported it."

Congress soon began to discuss ways to better regulate and control the NSA's most aggressive data collection practices. Even so, it took two years for Congress to pass legislation to reform the NSA's operations. After active debates in the House and the Senate, the USA FREEDOM Act (standing for the Uniting and Strengthening America by Fulfilling Rights and Ending Eavesdropping, Dragnet-Collection, and Online Monitoring Act) was signed into law on June 2, 2015.

Among its provisions, the bill banned the bulk collection of Americans' telephone records and internet metadata, imposed reporting requirements to FISA authorities, ended excessive secrecy of FISA court proceedings, and introduced advocate positions to represent the public's interests.

The bill has been criticized both for going too far and not going far enough. It also has been welcomed as a starting point for more reform. Jameel Jaffer, deputy legal director for the American Civil Liberties Union, says the FREEDOM Act is "the most important surveillance reform bill since 1978, and its passage is an indication that Americans are no longer willing to give the intelligence agencies a blank check."

can sometimes make potential whistleblowers afraid to come forward.

Despite the obstacles, Snowden decided to risk everything by contacting Greenwald and Poitras.

Whistleblower?

As Snowden's revelations became known, many critics questioned why he fled from the country before leaking the documents. They argued that if Snowden was truly acting as a whistleblower and exposing illegal activity, as he claimed, he should have remained in the United States and followed proper procedures that had already been established for these kinds of cases, including making his objections known to the higher levels of government charged with regulating the NSA and other security agencies.

Unlike civil disobedience, which involves a person resisting laws that already exist in an effort to change them, Snowden's critics said that whistleblowers are protected by law when they expose unlawful activities in the government and other organizations.

Snowden had reasons for not trusting the whistleblower process, however. Daniel Ellsberg tried to go through official channels when he exposed government deception during the Vietnam War (see chapter 1), but his information was ignored. Worse, he was then charged with espionage, and the government attempted to discredit him by stealing his personal information.

Ellsberg was not the only leaker to experience that kind of response.

Thomas Drake (*right*) was charged with espionage in 2010 after reporting problems within the NSA.

Thomas Drake

After spending ten years in the United States Air Force, Thomas Drake joined the NSA in 2001, focused on improving efficiency in their operations and programs. Drake became convinced that an NSA program called "Trailblazer" was collecting too many personal communications between ordinary Americans. He felt it violated the Fourth Amendment, which prohibited arbitrary searches and seizures. He also thought that it was too expensive and inefficient, and that a better system was already available.

Using the established framework for government whistleblowers, Drake voiced his concerns to his immediate bosses, but they dismissed his complaints. Drake then went to the NSA inspector general and the Pentagon, and he later testified to the House and Senate committees in charge of oversight. When nothing changed, Drake decided to leak his evidence to a local newspaper, the *Baltimore Sun*.

After the *Sun* and other papers published the story, the FBI raided Drake's home. Drake was later prosecuted for espionage and faced a potential penalty of thirty-five years in prison. The case against him eventually collapsed, but only after a long legal battle. Drake eventually pleaded guilty to a single misdemeanor for exceeding the authorized use of a computer and was sentenced to 250 hours of community service. However, his career, savings, and marriage suffered, and he had to take a job at an Apple store.

Chelsea Manning

US Army private Chelsea Manning leaked millions of pages of war logs about the action in Iraq and Afghanistan to the online site WikiLeaks. Manning managed to access classified government networks and obtained documents and files more than one hundred times the volume of the Pentagon Papers, which she burned onto CDs. Manning gave WikiLeaks more than 250,000 State Department cables, 500,000 US Army incident reports, dossiers on terrorist suspects detained at Guantánamo Bay, and videos of two air strikes that killed civilians in Iraq and Afghanistan.

Manning was arrested in 2010 after a hacker she trusted informed the authorities. Manning was sentenced to thirty-five years in prison in August 2013. President Obama commuted all but four months of her sentence before leaving office in January 2017, so she was to be released that May.

Support from Left and Right

When Snowden's first revelations were published, many politicians criticized both the leaks and the leaker. Many others expressed their support, however. Defenders came from both the left and the right, linking both sides of political expression.

Former congressman and presidential candidate Ron Paul said the US should be grateful for Snowden speaking out about the "injustice" carried out by the government. His son Rand, a senator from Kentucky who has also run for the presidential nomination of the Republican Party, described the NSA programs as "an all-out assault on the constitution."

Gordon Humphrey, a former two-term Republican senator from New Hampshire, wrote Snowden a letter in which he said:

> Provided you have not leaked information that would put in harm's way any intelligence agent, I believe you have done the right thing in exposing what I regard as [a] massive violation of the United States Constitution.

Humphrey also called Snowden "a courageous whistleblower" who had unearthed the "growing arrogance of our government."

Former President Jimmy Carter said that Snowden "obviously violated the laws of America, for which he's responsible, but I think the invasion of human rights and

American privacy has gone too far." Former Attorney General Eric Holder, once a fierce critic, has since acknowledged that Snowden performed a "public service."

Director Oliver Stone, who released the movie *Snowden* in late 2016, said, "To me [Snowden] is a hero because he revealed secrets that we all should know." Liberal film director Michael Moore labeled Snowden "Hero of the Year," while conservative commentator Glenn Beck said "I think I have

Many people praised Edward Snowden after his leaks became public.

just read about the man for which I have waited. Earmarks of a real hero."

More than three years later, the debate rages on.

Pardon Snowden?

Margaret Sullivan is a media columnist for the *Washington Post* and a former public editor for the *New York Times* and editor in chief of the *Buffalo News*. In September 2016, she wrote an article calling on President Obama to **pardon** Snowden before he leaves office. To support the case for a pardon, Sullivan summarizes many of the issues that Snowden's supporters raise in his defense:

> Snowden did an important—and brave—service for the American public and, in fact, the world, when he made it possible for news organizations to reveal widespread government surveillance of citizens. Some of that surveillance broke the law; some, although within the law, was nevertheless outrageous and unacceptable. And, afterward, some of the wrongs were righted through legislative reform …
>
> And notably … Snowden worked through journalists, rather than publish documents en masse himself, because he wanted the information to be carefully handled and responsibly vetted. He has been critical, in recent weeks, of WikiLeaks because of that organization's reckless just-publish-everything mentality. In other words, Snowden acted carefully, responsibly and courageously—and squarely in the public interest.

Sullivan also argues that "the president himself declared ... national debate [about the NSA's programs] important and worthwhile, although he criticized Snowden for breaking the law in making the classified documents public." And while he may have broken the law, Sullivan compares his actions to those of Daniel Ellsberg, who pointed out that "there was a more important obligation at work." While they both signed a standard secrecy agreement as a condition of employment, Ellsberg said that "their oath to defend the Constitution rightly took precedence."

Sullivan ends her argument by writing:

Snowden made it possible for journalists to provide a historic public service to his country. And his country ought to show him some appreciation, not threaten him with imprisonment or keep him in exile.

President Obama did not pardon Snowden before leaving office. In addition to commuting the sentence of Chelsea Manning, he pardoned James E. Cartright. Cartright, a retired Marine general and former vice chairman of the Joint Chiefs of Staff, had pleaded guilty to lying to the FBI about leaking classified information to reporters concerning cyberattacks on Iran's nuclear program.

Director of National Intelligence James Clapper defended US surveillance programs in the wake of Edward Snowden's leaks.

CHAPTER 3

Criticisms and Accusations

Snowden's revelations immediately embarrassed the US government. Not only were secret NSA operations made public; most government officials did not even know the programs existed at all. Many feared that America's safety and military personnel had been placed in grave danger and that security operations had been compromised. News that the NSA routinely intercepted their electronic communications upset world leaders around the globe, including staunch allies of the United States.

The US government reacted quickly to the Snowden leaks. On June 7, barely two days after the first *Guardian* article, Director of National Intelligence James Clapper released a statement basically admitting the existence of certain NSA spying programs. However, Clapper went on to defend the surveillance and instead criticized the leaks, saying, "The unauthorized disclosure about this important and entirely legal program is reprehensible and risks important protections for the security of Americans."

That same day, President Obama told the press that, when he first became president, he was wary about the NSA's eavesdropping program, but that he was convinced it was justified. "I came in with a healthy skepticism about these programs. My team evaluated them. We scrubbed them thoroughly. We actually expanded some of the oversight, increased some of [the] safeguards. But my assessment and my team's assessment was that they help us prevent terrorist attacks."

The US government formally indicted Snowden for espionage on June 21, less than two weeks after he revealed his identity. Snowden faced a long prison term if he was caught, tried, and found guilty.

The Route to Russia

Edward Snowden had arrived in Hong Kong on May 20 and was still there as the first newspaper stories appeared. Hong Kong's political situation is complicated; it is a part of China, but it also operates **autonomously** in many ways. After Snowden identified himself, America pressured officials in both Hong Kong and China to turn him over to US authorities. Despite repeated US requests, Snowden was permitted to leave Hong Kong, and he boarded a plane for Russia on June 23.

Ecuador's government had issued a certificate to Snowden that requested his safe conduct through other countries. Ecuador had previously granted political **asylum** to WikiLeaks founder Julian Assange. Snowden intended to travel from Hong Kong to Moscow, then leave for Cuba on his way to Ecuador. However, the US revoked Snowden's **passport** after he took off from Hong Kong, which meant that Snowden could not continue his travel once he landed in Russia.

President Vladimir Putin of Russia reportedly was not thrilled by Snowden's arrival, describing his presence as "an unwanted Christmas gift." However, Russia permitted Snowden to stay in the transit area of Moscow's Sheremetyevo International Airport. The United States then asked Russia to deliver Snowden into American hands. At first Russia refused, asserting that Snowden was still in a transit area of the airport and had not yet officially entered Russia. Then they claimed that Russia and the United States did not have an official **extradition** agreement in place. In the meantime, the United States managed to convince Ecuador to revoke its safe conduct pass. With Ecuador no longer an option and with no passport to permit further travel, Snowden was effectively stranded in Russia.

By July 1, Snowden had applied for asylum in twenty-one countries, including Russia. He claimed that pressure from the United States blocked his applications and left him as a "stateless person." As Snowden waited, Putin said that he could stay in Russia, but only if he would stop doing work that hurt Russia's "American partners." Secretly, Putin may have enjoyed putting the United States in a difficult position, but he also seemed concerned that the Snowden issue was further hurting his relationship with the United States, already strained due to many other international issues.

On August 1, 2013, Snowden was granted a temporary residency permit in Russia for one year. In 2014, his permit was extended for three more years, and in early 2017 for several more years. At that time Snowden still had no permanent home, while the debate over the effects of his leaks and whether he should be penalized continued to rage.

Groundswell of Criticism

As already mentioned, people from all sides of the political spectrum rose up to defend Snowden as soon as the leaks became public. His actions provoked equally emotional responses from his critics. Passionate attacks on Snowden's character, his motives, and the damage he caused to American security began to flow from both the right and the left, including powerful politicians as well as commentators and citizens.

РОССИЯ 24

Edward Snowden remains in Russia as America continues to debate his fate.

Right from the start, many accused Snowden of being self-centered and looking for attention. CBS News host Bob Schieffer called Snowden a "**narcissistic** young man" who thinks "he is smarter than the rest of us." Others focused on the fact that he "dropped out of high school," labeling him an antisocial computer nerd who was too naïve to understand how the real world worked.

As people learned more about Snowden, his background, and his roles at the NSA and CIA, the charges became more specific. The criticisms encompassed many different themes: that Snowden broke the law and lied, that he jeopardized America's security by revealing necessary surveillance programs, that he was in fact a traitor and not a whistleblower, and that he damaged America's reputation and influence around the world.

Laws and Oaths

Snowden claimed that the documents he leaked showed that the NSA and other security organizations failed to follow laws that were put in place to protect Americans' privacy. While some argue that the NSA programs were lawful and/or useful, others say that it doesn't matter. Whatever the legality of the NSA surveillance programs, Snowden revealed them, and that is against the law.

Snowden's critics point out that Snowden was initially very supportive of the NSA, and very critical of leakers, when he began working. They believe that his quick change of opinion after joining the government proves he is not consistent and does not think things through.

As a government employee, Snowden had sworn an oath of confidentiality. As a contractor working with the NSA,

The headquarters of the National Security Agency occupy two high-rise office buildings at Fort Meade, Maryland.

Snowden had also signed confidentiality contracts with his employers. He agreed not to reveal anything he encountered or learned while working on top-secret projects.

After leaving the CIA, Snowden worked for Dell, which performed work for the NSA. Snowden then left Dell and transferred to another NSA contractor, Booz Allen Hamilton. There, as a systems administrator, he could see any top-secret NSA file without anyone knowing. Snowden downloaded thousands of confidential files onto thumb drives, which in itself was illegal, and then left his office, never to return.

Snowden admits that he chose to leave Dell for Booz Allen Hamilton to get better access because he had already decided to steal and leak secret information. Snowden's accusers say that if he had stayed at the CIA or even Dell, he may have been able to claim that he decided to become a leaker after he started working. However, Snowden clearly and knowingly lied when he agreed to the same confidentiality policies at Booz Allen Hamilton, doing so only to carry out his plan to steal secret documents. Therefore, they charge, Snowden willfully violated all of those signed oaths and contracts. His actions were premeditated, they say, meaning that he knew in advance that he intended to violate his contractor agreements even before he signed them.

Not a Whistleblower

Some believe that Snowden's revelations about NSA surveillance make him a whistleblower. His opponents disagree.

A whistleblower is a person working within an organization who reports on that organization's misconduct. For people who work for the federal government, the Whistleblower Protection Enhancement Act, or WPEA, protects federal employees who disclose illegal or improper government activities. The WPEA prohibits the government from retaliating against any federal employee who reports a violation of any law, rule, or regulation, as well as mismanagement, waste, abuse of authority, or dangers to public health or safety.

However, the WPEA requires that the whistleblower disclose the problem to higher levels of government, including a supervisor, upper management, a member of Congress, or a congressional committee. Also, the WPEA specifies that the disclosure must not be prohibited by law and cannot include information that needs to be kept secret in the interest of national defense or the conduct of foreign affairs.

Snowden's critics argue that he did not try to report the NSA's activities to his superiors, and that the kinds of secret information that Snowden revealed are not covered by whistleblower statutes. More than three years later, in September 2016, White House press secretary Josh Earnest stated that the government still did not consider Edward Snowden to be a whistleblower. Earnest said:

> There actually is a specific process that is well-established and well-protected that allows whistleblowers to raise concerns that they have, particularly when it relates to confidential or classified information, to do so in a way that protects the national security secrets of the United States. That is not what Mr. Snowden did. And his conduct put American lives at risk, and it risked American national security. And that's why the policy of the Obama administration is that Mr. Snowden should return to the United States and face the very serious charges that … he's facing. He will of course be afforded the rights that are due to every American citizen in our criminal justice system, but we believe that he should return to the United States and face those charges.

Like Ellsberg?

People also try to compare Snowden's actions to those of famous whistleblowers of the past like Daniel Ellsberg. Snowden opponents point out, however, that the Ellsberg and Snowden cases were not the same in many important respects. In his book *The War on Leakers*, author Lloyd C. Gardner highlights many of the differences between Ellsberg and Snowden.

Ellsberg had studied politics and economics at Harvard University in the United States and Cambridge in England. He then served as a marine and spent two years in Vietnam. Ellsberg was a mature forty-year-old and a military veteran by the time he joined the US government as an advisor. He benefited from direct, regular contact with government officials at the highest levels, where he personally discussed complex subjects and heard both sides of any issue. He understood the needs for government secrecy and considered many sides.

When Ellsberg made his decision to copy and expose the Pentagon Papers, he did that only after thinking about it for a long period of time, and within the context of his years of experience in policy making. Even then, he first offered the documents to congressmen, who refused to take any action. When he released the documents, Ellsberg continued to live in the United States under public scrutiny, and he made himself subject to US laws, including a trial. And, in another important distinction, the Pentagon Papers only covered what had happened in the past. They did not contain any information about current US operations or plans for the war in Vietnam.

Snowden, on the other hand, was in his twenties with little real education or experience outside of technology. He worked for the government for a relatively short time, much of that as an outside contractor. He had no real insight into the complex issues involved, or any real contact or discussions with those responsible for establishing the policies and programs that Snowden felt objectionable.

When he made his decision to expose what he considered to be illegal surveillance and violations of privacy, Snowden did not follow established whistleblower procedures and did not attempt to raise his objections to his superiors and higher levels of government. Instead, he left the country before leaking his documents to the *Guardian* and other papers, and his presence in Russia does not allow public scrutiny and dialogue. Furthermore, Snowden exposed current NSA operations designed to keep Americans safe, and he continued to leak more details well after the debate over his revelations had begun. (Snowden claims his leaks stopped before he left Hong Kong. The reason news stories came out for a long time afterward is that reporters and editors were confirming the information and seeking reaction from other sources. This could have confused commentators who believed that he continued to leak information.)

Kept Talking

For some, Snowden's true motives come into question because it appeared that he kept releasing information and talking in public well after the initial newspaper articles were published. If the point was to expose the extent of NSA surveillance and start the discussion, why keep talking and leaking once that was accomplished?

William H. Harwood, a philosophy instructor for the University of Texas–Pan American, wrote a column for the *Huffington Post* in which he criticizes Snowden for continuing to leak specific details about programs he'd already exposed. Harwood stated:

> Any defense of Snowden ended when he kept talking. And, as if hell-bent on crushing all hope of redemption, he keeps providing details ... If we already knew that we were data-mining inconceivable amounts of information, not just on Americans but on everyone everywhere, the revelation of exactly on whom and by what means we spied offers delicious tidbits without providing any useful insights ... The important question has never been whether Snowden is a selfless patriot or a narcissistic nihilist. It is how we convince him to stop.

Not Civil Disobedience

Whether or not Snowden qualifies as a whistleblower, supporters also suggest that he also was practicing "civil disobedience," a peaceful method of political protest and resistance, to rightfully challenge the NSA's actions. Famous nonviolent leaders of the past like Mahatma Gandhi and Martin Luther King Jr. had effectively employed civil disobedience as a means of changing government policy and promoting change.

Snowden's opponents disagree. They argue that true civil disobedience requires a person to accept the legal consequences for refusing to follow the laws she or he wants to change. For

Gandhi, nonviolent protest required "voluntary submission to the penalty of non-cooperation with evil." King said that accepting the legal consequences demonstrated respect for law and the legitimacy of order. By publicly accepting prosecution and even punishment, even if it is unjust, protesters have a better chance to change public opinion.

Snowden's detractors point to the fact that he fled the United States and refused to accept the legal penalties for his actions. In their minds, that disqualified Snowden as someone who might be practicing a form of civil disobedience, regardless of his justifications. If he wanted to change the law, or to accuse the NSA of breaking the law, then he had to demonstrate support for the concept of law by accepting the consequences as others had done in the past.

Not Everything Was Illegal

Putting aside Snowden's actions and turning attention to the leaks themselves and what they revealed, Snowden's opponents believe that the conversation about "illegal" NSA operations misses something important. They point out that many of the programs Snowden revealed were indeed legal, as well as necessary and effective in protecting American lives.

Author Fred Kaplan, who has often written about cybersecurity, wrote a column for *Slate* in September 2016 in which he says that Snowden's leaks identified important programs, including "the NSA's interception of email and cell phone calls by the Taliban in Pakistan's northwest territories; an operation to gauge the loyalties of CIA recruits in Pakistan; intelligence assessments inside Iran; and NSA surveillance of cell phone calls … [that] allows it to look for unknown associates of known intelligence targets by tracking people whose movements intersect." Snowden also disclosed that the NSA routinely hacks into hundreds of computers in China, Russia, and other hostile countries.

Kaplan goes on to write:

> Whatever one's views of US foreign policy in those parts of the world, these activities are legitimate aspects of the NSA's charter, which involves intercepting communications of foreign powers. They have nothing to do with domestic surveillance or spying on allies. Exposing these intercepts is not whistleblowing. It's an attempt to blow US intelligence operations. And while Snowden has since acknowledged that other countries do this sort of thing too, not least China and his host at the moment, Russia, he never leaked documents revealing their hacking programs even though, in his job at the NSA, he would have had access to reports (and possibly raw data) about them as well.

Kaplan claims that facts like these were not included in Oliver Stone's 2016 movie about Snowden, which he argues presented a biased and one-sided view about Snowden and his actions.

Lives at Risk

One of the major themes of Snowden's attackers is that his leaks exposed NSA security operations that were preventing terrorist attacks and saving lives. By making them public, Snowden damaged American security and put lives at risk. Even simply revealing that the programs existed put America's

Blocking a Terrorist Plot

Among the many components of the NSA surveillance program, one involved the collection of telephone metadata, which was authorized under Section 215 of the PATRIOT Act. Another used a separate program called PRISM, which intercepted internet traffic, including emails, and was authorized under Section 702 of the Foreign Intelligence Surveillance Act.

While little proof exists that the use of telephone metadata has actually prevented terrorist attacks, documented cases credit PRISM with thwarting terrorist plots. In September 2009, PRISM was credited with helping the FBI prevent a suicide bomb attack on the New York City subway system.

Najibullah Zazi was born in Afghanistan and raised in New York City. He traveled to Pakistan in 2008 to join the Taliban and fight Americans in Afghanistan. While there, he learned to make bombs and was recruited by al-Qaeda to return to the United States as a suicide bomber. He moved to Denver early in 2009 and planned to attack the subway in New York City in September, eight years after 9/11.

Government officials claim that using PRISM, the NSA intercepted emails between Zazi and an associate in Pakistan early in September that contained coded messages concerning the pending attack. An Associated Press report disputes that, saying the British found the email address on a laptop and gave the address to the United States, which then intercepted the emails. Regardless of how they were obtained, the emails were given to the FBI and proved crucial in helping identify Zazi and six coconspirators.

Najibullah Zazi pleaded guilty to terrorism charges in 2010 after plotting to attack the New York City subway system.

Now under surveillance, Zazi drove to New York City with homemade explosives. When his car was stopped on the George Washington Bridge but then let go, Zazi feared he had been discovered and drove back to Denver, where he was arrested on September 19. Zazi pleaded guilty to terrorism charges in February 2010. The six others were also convicted.

Attorney General Eric Holder called the attack planned by Zazi and others in his group "one of the most serious terrorist threats to our nation since September 11, 2001."

enemies on guard about using communications methods that the NSA might be able to monitor and analyze.

Snowden's supporters claim that the NSA has not presented any real evidence that their massive electronic surveillance programs really saved American lives or prevented terrorist attacks. Indeed, a review panel commissioned by the White House reported in December 2014 that the telephone metadata collection program—performed under Section 215 of the PATRIOT Act—had made "only a modest contribution to the nation's security." The report said that "there has been no instance in which [the] NSA could say with confidence that the outcome [of a terror investigation] would have been different" without the program.

Snowden's critics insist that there is a lot more to the story, however. The NSA surveillance program was extremely complex and had many parts. While some practices may have violated personal privacy or been difficult to justify, others were remarkably effective and valuable. Regarding another NSA program called PRISM, for example, the same White House panel stated that "the record is very impressive. It's no doubt the nation is safer and spared potential attacks because of [PRISM]."

Chancellor Angela Merkel of Germany acknowledged that intelligence sharing with the United States helped to prevent an Islamic terrorist plot in Germany in 2007.

Hurt US Relationships

Snowden's disclosures about extensive surveillance on foreign governments and leaders sparked angry reactions from America's allies.

Germany, in particular, had direct, recent experience with secret government surveillance. During World War II,

Nazi Germany used its secret police force, the Gestapo, to spy on its own people. At the end of the war, Germany was split into halves. East Germany, known at the German Democratic Republic (GDR), became a totalitarian state under the influence of the Soviet Union. The GDR's Ministry for State Security—the Stasi—functioned as a secret intelligence agency and political secret police that also used secret electronic surveillance to spy on its own citizens who opposed the government.

News that the NSA spied on Chancellor Angela Merkel of Germany (*right*) affected her relationship with President Barack Obama.

When East Germany collapsed and merged back into a united free Germany, the backlash against secret government spying was strong. The new constitution stressed the right to privacy. Given their history, Germans reacted strongly when Snowden's documents revealed widespread US spying inside their country. The NSA had even tapped Merkel's phone for ten years. Merkel was perhaps the most powerful politician in Europe at the time and a staunch US ally. She had also grown up in the GDR and knew firsthand about living in a police state.

In an interview with the *Guardian* and other European newspapers, Merkel described the scandal as "extremely serious." Allegations of the NSA bugging her mobile phone reportedly left her "livid."

France was angry as well and summoned the US ambassador to explain the NSA actions. Brazil felt the spying was a violation of its sovereignty, and its president, Dilma Rousseff, canceled a scheduled visit to the United States. That September, Rousseff gave a speech to the United Nations during which she said that the American "global network of electronic spying" had caused worldwide anger, was an affront to relations between friendly states, and was a breach of international law.

America's global reputation was severely harmed. President Obama had been extremely popular in Europe before the Snowden files were revealed. Afterward, Europeans questioned America's motives and whether the United States could be trusted. The German magazine *Stern* labeled President Obama as "the informer" on one of its cover stories after the leaks.

Helping the Enemy

Snowden's critics also viewed his travel with suspicion. When Snowden left Hawaii, he flew first to Hong Kong, a Chinese territory, and then to Russia. Neither China nor Russia is allied with America, and much of the US surveillance effort is directed against those countries.

Snowden's critics questioned why he chose those two countries to hide in. Did the Chinese or the Russians gain access to sensitive documents? Was Snowden secretly working with either country, or both? Was he now cooperating with Russia in return for being permitted to remain?

Snowden denies that he shared any files with China or Russia, and he maintains that his encryption makes it impossible for any country to steal usable information from him. Snowden continues to live in Russia, however, which

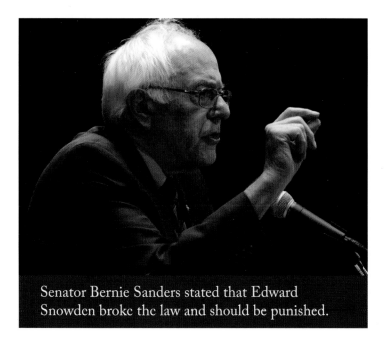

Senator Bernie Sanders stated that Edward Snowden broke the law and should be punished.

also practices electronic surveillance but without any of the controls that exist in America. Russia could also revoke his residency at any time, leaving Snowden with nowhere to go except the United States. Some fear that Russia's leverage over Snowden may force him to help them in ways that could harm America. Suspicion will remain as long as Snowden lives outside the United States.

The Need for Secrecy

For some people, the question of whether to punish Snowden or not comes down to one broader, practical issue: If he is not penalized or punished, what can prevent anyone else in government or the private sector from also violating promises of confidentiality or privacy based on their own opinions? How could governments function without any expectation of internal commitment or trust, especially in such sensitive areas as national security?

Snowden's detractors argue that, in order for America's intelligence and diplomatic organizations to work, they need to be able to operate in secret, having conversations and establishing programs that, if revealed, could damage American interests. To accomplish that, the NSA must be able to rely on government employees and contractors not to expose what they worked on or came into contact with. Snowden broke his commitment to safeguard a wide variety of secrets that he had sworn to protect.

At a Vermont town hall meeting in February 2014, Senator Bernie Sanders raised that point when talking about Snowden, saying, "Look, you don't want to have a situation where everybody who works for the government suddenly wakes up and says, 'You know, I think I've gotta reveal this information despite any oath or agreement that I made.' You're gonna have chaos."

Sanders continued, "He broke the law. I think that clearly … there should be an effort to enter into a plea agreement." Sanders did say later that he thought "what [Snowden] did in educating us should be taken into consideration," but what he did was still illegal and should be punished.

Secretary of State John Kerry (*right*) called Edward Snowden a coward and a traitor and challenged him to return to the United States to face charges.

Kerry: "Coward and Traitor"

Many others agreed with Sanders. John Kerry, the secretary of state in the second Obama administration, condemned Snowden and his actions during interviews with MSNBC and CBS in May 2014, nearly one year after the Snowden leaks were published. In his comments, Kerry summarized many of the arguments that people had been raising for many months against Snowden, his motives, and his actions.

"Edward Snowden is a coward," Kerry said. "He is a traitor. And he has betrayed his country. And if he wants to come home tomorrow to face the music, he can do so."

Kerry admitted that the now-international debate about privacy and the NSA would not have risen to such a high level without Snowden's disclosures. However, Kerry insisted that these same issues were important to President Obama before Snowden's leaks, and he said the disclosures imperiled national security. "More importantly, much more importantly, what he's done is hurt his country," Kerry said. "What he's done is expose, for terrorists, a lot of mechanisms which now affect operational security of those terrorists and make it harder for the United States to break up plots, harder to protect our nation."

Kerry criticized Snowden for fleeing to an authoritarian country like Russia. He challenged the NSA leaker to return to the United States to "make his case" to the American public:

He should man up, come back to the United States. If he has a complaint about what's wrong with American surveillance, come back here and stand in our system of justice and make his case. But instead, he's just sitting there taking pot shots at his country, violating his oath that he took when he took on the job he took, and betraying, I think, the fundamental agreement that he entered into when he became an employee.

Interestingly, Kerry had served in Vietnam as a naval officer, winning a Bronze Star and a Silver Star for heroism, as well as three Purple Hearts for being wounded in battle. During his tour, however, Kerry became increasingly disenchanted, and in 1971 he testified before Congress about war crimes committed in Vietnam by Americans. At the time, when he was criticized for speaking publicly about what he saw, Kerry responded, "We could come back to this country, we could be quiet, we could hold our silence, we could not tell what went on in Vietnam, but we feel, because of what threatens this country, not the Reds [communists], but the crimes which we are committing that threaten it, that we have to speak out."

When he ran for president in 2004, opponents accused Kerry of lying and of being a traitor for exposing secret US actions in Vietnam. While some tried to compare Snowden's actions to Kerry's, Kerry did remain in the country, and he testified publicly at official government hearings. Kerry challenged Snowden to do the same.

Rejecting a Petition for Pardon

As discussions about the Snowden affair continued to heat up, many of his supporters partnered to petition the White House to grant him a pardon and allow him to return home with no punishment. They used an online White House platform called "We the People," which helps Americans easily create a petition online and share it to solicit the public's support. If the petition attracts one hundred thousand signatures within thirty days, it is shown to the appropriate policy experts. The site then posts an official government response.

The online petition for Snowden's pardon was submitted with nearly 168,000 signatures. The official response made it clear that the US government did not intend to pardon Snowden at that time:

A Response to Your Petition on Edward Snowden

Thanks for signing a petition about Edward Snowden. This is an issue that many Americans feel strongly about. Because his actions have had serious consequences for our national security, we took this matter to Lisa Monaco, the President's Advisor on Homeland Security and Counterterrorism. Here's what she had to say:

"Since taking office, President Obama has worked with Congress to secure appropriate reforms that balance the protection of civil liberties with the ability of national security professionals to secure information vital to keep Americans safe.

"As the President said in announcing recent intelligence reforms, 'We have to make some important decisions about how to protect ourselves and sustain our leadership in the world, while upholding the civil liberties and privacy protections that our ideals and our Constitution require.'

"Instead of constructively addressing these issues, Mr. Snowden's dangerous decision to steal and disclose classified information had severe consequences for the security of our country and the people who work day in and day out to protect it.

"If he felt his actions were consistent with civil disobedience, then he should do what those who have taken issue with their own government do: Challenge it, speak out, engage in a constructive act of protest, and—importantly—accept the consequences of his actions. He should come home to the United States, and be judged by a jury of his peers—not hide behind the cover of an authoritarian regime. Right now, he's running away from the consequences of his actions. "We live in a dangerous world. We continue to face grave security threats like terrorism, cyber-attacks, and nuclear proliferation that our intelligence community must have all the lawful tools it needs to address. The balance between our security and the civil liberties that our ideals and our Constitution require deserves robust debate and those who are willing to engage in it here at home."

Author George Orwell coined the phrase "Big Brother is Watching You" to describe government spying in his classic novel *Nineteen Eighty-Four*.

CHAPTER 4

Privacy, Security, and Fears of Big Brother

n June 1949, not long after the end of World War II, George Orwell published his famous novel *Nineteen Eighty-Four*. In his book, Orwell described a future world where three totalitarian states engage in constant warfare. Citizens live under continuous electronic government surveillance, with spies everywhere and two-way television screens in every home. Orwell coined the phrase "Big Brother is watching you" to describe a time when every person, every action, and almost every thought is monitored by a mysterious, malevolent government (Big Brother) to control information and hold power.

While the calendar year 1984 passed more than thirty years ago, the future world that Orwell imagined can sometimes look all too real today. The war on terror seems never to end, and the government continues to expand and refine its electronic surveillance capabilities.

Besides the government, many other organizations and businesses employ their own forms of electronic surveillance. Companies like Facebook and Google collect vast amounts of data about their users, much of it voluntarily supplied by the people themselves. These companies track our likes and dislikes, our activities, our interests, and our movements, and share that information with advertisers. Banks and credit card companies monitor and store our financial data and transactions. Cable and telephone companies provide our connectivity to the world, all the while collecting our browsing histories and phone call records. In reality, little if anything we do today can really be done in secret.

Power to Prosecute

Despite the realization that protecting privacy may be difficult in today's connected world, the potential danger posed by secret government surveillance remains a major concern. While private companies may know some things about us, unchecked government surveillance could paint complete pictures of our lives. Plus, the government has the power to use our information in ways that companies could never duplicate. In a column for the *New York Times* in June 2013, retired executive editor Max Frankel wrote:

> We have long since surrendered a record of our curiosities and fantasies to Google. We have broadcast our tastes and addictions for the convenience of one-button Amazon shopping ... But Google and Amazon do not indict, jail and prosecute the people they track and bug. The issue ... is how to protect our civil liberty against the anxious pursuit of civic security. Our rights must not be so casually bartered as our Facebook chatter.

A New Era

While Snowden's actions sparked discussion about government surveillance and the balance between keeping the country safe versus the need for privacy, the subject itself is far from new. The debate has swung back and forth, like a pendulum, since the end of World War II.

Author Luke Harding describes America's recent history of security as consisting of four **epochs**. During the first epoch, which began with the founding of the NSA in 1952, the NSA operated without much attention or oversight as the country worried about the threat of communism. The second epoch began in 1978, when discoveries of domestic surveillance abuses by the FBI and CIA led to reforms and restrictions of NSA operations. The third began in 2001, when the tragedy of 9/11 led to a wave of fear and triggered a renewed commitment to secret and widespread surveillance. That lasted until 2013, the start of the fourth epoch, when Snowden's leaks caused America to once again question the government's extensive spying capabilities.

With that perspective, it's easy to understand why recent comments about Edward Snowden inspire a sense of "**déjà vu**," as they sound eerily similar to thoughts that were expressed back in 1978, when massive government overreach was also exposed.

The Church Committee

During the 1970s, disclosures about government lies regarding Vietnam and secret spying by the FBI and CIA led people to mistrust how the government used its powers. In response, the Senate established the Unites States Senate

Senator Frank Church led a Senate committee that investigated US intelligence abuses in 1975.

Select Committee to Study Governmental Operations with Respect to Intelligence Activities in 1975, the first public investigation of American's intelligence agencies. Chaired by Senator Frank Church of Idaho, the Church Committee, as it was commonly called, exposed surveillance abuses during televised hearings.

The Church Committee believed the nation would benefit from an honest examination of the facts. It released a statement that read in part:

Despite our distaste for what we have seen, we have great faith in this country. The story is sad, but this country has the strength to hear the story and to learn from it. We must remain a people who confront our mistakes and resolve not to repeat them. If we do not, we will decline; but, if we do, our future will be worthy of the best of our past.

Senator Church warned that the NSA's capabilities were so great that, if the agency turned on the American people, "there would be no place to hide." Church said the NSA had the power to "make tyranny total in America."

The technology that Church feared back in 1975 was primitive by today's standards. Snowden's exposure of current NSA surveillance programs has led to the same kind of self-examination that Senator Church talked about more than four decades ago.

Looking for Balance

In August 2013, two months after the first newspaper articles appeared, President Obama appointed a group of experts to investigate all the issues raised by Snowden. Obama wanted to know how the United States could continue to use technology to protect national security while preventing further leaks. However, the president also wanted to respect privacy and civil liberties, and maintain the public trust. To many people, those goals seemed contradictory and perhaps even impossible.

The group reported its findings in December 2013. Its recommendations included ending the metadata program and changing the way the secret Foreign Intelligence Surveillance Court operated.

The report did help to propel serious discussion inside and outside of government about how to reform surveillance practices to strike a better balance between the need for security and the responsibility to follow the Constitution and protect citizens' rights. The fact that some security polices, including parts of the PATRIOT Act, were soon due to expire helped provide further context. After many stops and starts, Congress finally passed the USA FREEDOM Act in June 2015 (see chapter 2).

Conflicted Emotions

Passage of the USA FREEDOM Act did not satisfy everyone. Some felt it went too far in restricting surveillance capabilities and that it put the Unites States at a disadvantage against its enemies. Others said it did not go far enough, fearing that the government continued to secretly collect too much personal information and that its power could still be used against citizens.

Many others felt themselves caught in the middle. They believed that we needed to protect ourselves from our enemies, but they knew about past government abuses of power and remained concerned about government overreach. Their feelings of **ambivalence** extended to opinions about Edward Snowden as well.

Politicians Shift

Former NSA head Michael Hayden told an interviewer that he was "conflicted" over the issue of leaks about US government electronic wiretapping. The topic under discussion was whether *New York Times* reporter James Risen should be prosecuted for failing to reveal his sources for a

Senator Dianne Feinstein changed her opinion about Edward Snowden after learning more about the NSA surveillance programs.

story on a failed CIA attempt to undermine Iran's nuclear program. While he still believed that leaks to newspapers damaged the government's ability to protect Americans, Hayden also did not want to harm freedom of the press. "The government needs to be strong enough to keep me safe, but I don't want it so strong that it threatens my liberties," Hayden said. Former Attorney General Eric Holder, once a fierce Snowden critic, has also acknowledged that Snowden performed a "public service."

Senator Dianne Feinstein of California, vice-chair of the Senate committee that oversees US intelligence, first condemned Snowden. "I don't look at this as being a whistleblower," she said. "I think it's an act of treason. He violated the oath. He violated the law." However, after learning more about the leaks, including that Chancellor Angela Merkel's personal phone was hacked, Feinstein demanded a "'total review" of all intelligence programs and said that she was "totally opposed" to spying on foreign leaders who were US allies.

Americans themselves seemed conflicted. One poll showed that more than half of the population (54 percent) approved of Snowden's leaks, but nearly 72 percent also believed he should be prosecuted. Another poll indicated that Americans seemed to be more sympathetic to him than to previous leakers and believed that Snowden was more whistleblower than traitor.

Confusion at the *Post*

Perhaps no case exemplifies these mixed feelings more than the contradictory opinions published by the *Washington Post*. The *Post* was one of the first newspapers to work closely with

Snowden and publish the Snowden leaks, and it later won a **Pulitzer Prize** along with the *Guardian* for its coverage. Years later, however, the paper's editorial board published an opinion on September 17, 2016, that favored prosecuting Snowden rather than pardoning him. While much of what Snowden did was justified and valuable, they said, Snowden

Washington Post reporter Barton Gellman won a Pulitzer Prize for stories about the NSA based on Edward Snowden's information.

also "pilfered, and leaked, information about a separate overseas NSA [program] ... that was both clearly legal and not clearly threatening to privacy ... Worse—far worse—he also leaked details of basically defensible international intelligence operations."

While many newspapers have long separated their news operations from their editorial board, the contradiction between the *Post*'s reporting on Snowden and its editorial position led many to question the paper's integrity, especially since it had accepted journalism's greatest honor for its Snowden coverage.

Mathew Ingram, a senior writer for *Fortune* magazine, said that "All that outside observers are likely to see at this point is a newspaper at war with itself ... happy to take the leaks and win prizes for them and then just as happy to throw its source under a bus." The *Post*'s own media columnist, Margaret Sullivan, wrote that the paper "won the Pulitzer Prize for public service for stories made possible by Snowden's leak ... Some see it, then, as hypocritical for [the *Post*'s] editorial board to weigh in against a pardon."

Secrecy Versus the Law

Few question that some government secrets are legitimate and necessary to protect American citizens. However, that does not dismiss the Constitution's requirement to protect personal rights and the rule of law.

President Obama acknowledged the extreme importance of that discussion when he said, "Given the history of abuse by governments, it's right to ask questions about surveillance—particularly as technology is reshaping every aspect of our lives." He went on further to state, "Our system of government is based on the premise that our liberty cannot depend on the good intentions of those in power. It depends on the law to constrain those in power."

President Obama also talked about the conflict between secrecy and the law, and the need for laws to keep up with the speed of technological development. In January 2014 he said:

Intelligence agencies cannot function without secrecy … Yet there is an inevitable bias not only within the intelligence community, but among all of us who are responsible for national security, to collect more information about the world, not less. So, in the absence of … regular debate—and oversight that is public, as well as private or classified—the danger of government overreach becomes more acute. And this is particularly true when surveillance technology and our reliance on digital information is evolving much faster than our laws.

Aftermath

It took just a day or two before Snowden's leaks sparked worldwide reaction. The effects continue today.

Just days after the first *Guardian* article, James Clapper, the director of national intelligence, had to apologize for deceiving Congress about spying on Americans. In quick succession, General Keith Alexander, the director of the NSA, was exposed for falsely telling Congress that the NSA did not hold data on US citizens. Two courts criticized the NSA and its lawyers for lying to the court. Alexander left the NSA in March 2014.

Some governments began to back off modern electronic communications by using notes written by hand and typewriter, and by conducting personal conversations outside of their offices rather than by phone. Technology companies took steps to protect their resources from outside surveillance and to restore trust in their services. For example, Microsoft announced plans to open transparency centers where foreign governments could inspect the company's code and make sure that it does not plant back doors that spies could access.

Germany's Angela Merkel later called for a new framework to regulate spying between partners. Many European countries have since voted for new and tougher rules regarding data privacy. Countries also began working on something they called "cyber-sovereignty," which meant greater state control of the internet in their own countries in order to make it harder for the United States to get access to data. Those efforts could turn the universal internet into something that becomes fragmented and different in each country.

No Permanent Home

Where is Snowden today? Will he ever be allowed to come back to the United States?

As of this writing, Edward Snowden still lives in Russia, relying on residency permits granted periodically by the Russian government. His girlfriend, Lindsay Mills, joined him there in July 2014. Snowden's US-based lawyer reports that Snowden leads a relatively free life in Russia, making appearances via live video and even publishing articles against Russia's human rights violations.

Snowden has received several awards for leaking information about NSA surveillance. One, the Sam Adams Award, was presented by an organization of former national security officials in honor of Samuel A. Adams, a member of the CIA who challenged the Pentagon for issuing false information during the Vietnam War. Snowden also won the Ridenhour Prize for Truth Telling.

Oliver Stone released his movie *Snowden* in September 2016. Snowden appears as himself in a short scene at the end, during which he says, "I no longer have to worry about what happens tomorrow, because I'm happy with what I've done today."

Snowden still says he would like to come home the United States, but only if he could face a fair trial. On November 8, 2016, Donald Trump was elected to succeed Barack Obama as president of the United States, making it even more unclear what the future may hold for Edward Snowden.

The Digital Challenge

The future of electronic surveillance remains unclear as well. The international battle over controlling cyberspace continues to rage. Hostile governments, as well as terrorist groups, are becoming increasingly aggressive in terms of using technology to steal information and disrupt infrastructures and computer networks around the world, all without the legal constraints that bind the United States and other western democracies.

Today we live in a truly digital world that offers virtually limitless capabilities to collect, store, and disseminate huge amounts of personal information. The future promises even more connectivity, with the "internet of things" (IOT) linking household appliances, personal devices, and automobiles into

Unable to leave Russia, Edward Snowden uses internet video links to speak at conferences around the world.

an ever-expanding electronic network, providing more and more detail about how we live and what we think.

Technology allows the government to collect, store, and use more information than ever before. That same technology empowers individual people to access sensitive data and spread it to the world via the internet and sites like WikiLeaks, rather than depend on news organizations and other traditional means of reporting. In spite of these developments, many government and oversight policies date back to the days of paper, pen, and typewriters.

Is it possible that there is truth to both sides of the discussion about secrecy versus safety? Was Snowden right in leaking the NSA information? Should he still be punished?

The discussion continues, encompassing all levels of political, legal, ethical, and philosophical thought. In many ways, Snowden has succeeded in the mission he committed to when he decided to steal secret NSA surveillance data just a few short years ago.

Now Edward Snowden waits to see what the future holds, both for him and for the world.

June 21, 1983 Edward Snowden is born in Elizabeth City, North Carolina.

2006 Snowden joins the Central Intelligence Agency (CIA).

March 2007–February 2009 Snowden works in Geneva, Switzerland, under diplomatic cover as an IT and cybersecurity expert for the CIA, where he becomes disillusioned with what he sees.

2009–2012 Snowden works for Dell as a contractor. He does work for the NSA and the CIA, including moving to an NSA facility in Japan.

March 2012 Snowden moves to Hawaii as a Dell contractor working for the NSA. He later leaves Dell to join another contractor, Booz Allen Hamilton.

December 1, 2012 Snowden first makes anonymous contact with *Guardian* journalist Glenn Greenwald.

May 2013 Snowden takes temporary leave from his consultant position with the NSA in Hawaii.

May 20, 2013 Snowden arrives in Hong Kong.

June 1, 2013 Snowden meets with Greenwald, fellow *Guardian* journalist Ewen MacAskill, and documentary filmmaker Laura Poitras.

June 5, 2013 The *Guardian* publishes its first exclusive story based on Snowden's leaks, revealing a secret court order showing that the US government had forced the telecom giant Verizon to hand over the phone records of millions of Americans.

June 9, 2013 The *Guardian* reveals Edward Snowden's identity at his request. Director of National Intelligence James Clapper condemns Snowden's actions as having done "huge, grave damage" to US intelligence capabilities.

June 23, 2013 Snowden flies to Russia from Hong Kong.

June 28, 2013 Ecuador withdraws Snowden's safe conduct pass.

January 1, 2014 The *New York Times* recommends clemency for Snowden, or at least "substantially reduced punishment," writing that while he may have broken the law, he had "done his country a great service" by bringing the abuses of the NSA to light.

February 16, 2014 Journalists Glenn Greenwald, Laura Poitras, Ewen MacAskill, and the *Washington Post's* Barton Gellman are honored with a 2013 George Polk Award for Journalism, which they dedicate to Snowden.

April 14, 2014 The *Guardian* and the *Washington Post* win the 2014 Pulitzer Prize for Public Service for their reporting on the Snowden documents.

May 7, 2015 In the case of *ACLU v. Clapper*, the United States Court of Appeals says that Section 215 of the PATRIOT Act did not authorize the NSA to collect Americans' calling records in bulk, as revealed by Snowden in 2013.

June 2, 2015 US Congress passes the USA FREEDOM Act.

September 17, 2016 The editorial board of the *Washington Post* argues against a presidential pardon for Edward Snowden, even though the paper won a Pulitzer Prize for its reporting on the leaks, for which Snowden was their source. The decision puts the board in opposition with its own reporting staff.

ambivalence Contradictory or uncertain feelings, such as agreement and disagreement, that are experienced simultaneously by one person.

asylum A place for protection and shelter, sometimes granted by countries to a person who is being persecuted or pursued by the government of another country.

autonomously The ability to make decisions independently without any outside interference.

blogged Adding new material to a "blog," a regularly updated website or web page, typically run by an individual or small group, that is written in an informal or conversational style.

CIA The Central Intelligence Agency, a civilian foreign intelligence service of the United States federal government, which gathers and analyzes national security information from around the world.

classified A designation of information created or received by an agency of the federal government or a government contractor that, in the interest of national security, must be protected against disclosure.

contractor A person who is hired to perform work for another company. Some contractors work for companies outside the government but do government work. Some perform work for the United States outside of the country.

counterintelligence Government activity meant to hide the truth from an enemy or to prevent the enemy from learning secret information.

cyberspace The online world of computer networks and the internet.

déjà vu A feeling that someone has seen or heard something before.

documentary A movie or other program that presents a factual report about a person or an event.

encrypted A process of converting emails, files, or any other data to an unrecognizable form to protect sensitive information so that only certain authorized people can view it.

epochs Periods of time in history that are usually marked by important events.

espionage Spying to obtain information about the plans and activities of a foreign government or a competing company.

extradition To give up or send a person to another country at its request.

FBI The Federal Bureau of Investigation, the domestic intelligence and security service of the United States. It also serves as the nation's primary federal law enforcement agency.

hacked A term that describes when a computer is used to gain unauthorized access to data in a system.

leak When someone discloses secret information to a person or organization not authorized to receive that information.

manga A Japanese-based style of graphic novel or comic book characterized by highly stylized art. Different types are intended for adults or children.

metadata Information that provides details about other information. For example, an image may include metadata that describes how large the picture is, its resolution, and when the image was created. A text document's metadata may contain information about its length, who wrote it and when, and a short summary.

narcissistic A person having an excessive or inflated sense of his or her own importance.

NSA The National Security Agency, an intelligence organization of the United States government, responsible for global monitoring, collection, and processing of information and data for foreign intelligence and counterintelligence purposes.

Nuremberg Tribunal A series of trials that took place in Nuremberg, Germany, between 1945 and 1949 for the purpose of bringing Nazi war criminals to justice.

pardon The right of the US president to forgive someone for a crime or to excuse someone from a punishment.

passport An official document issued by a government that identifies someone as a citizen and that is needed to enter or leave any country.

Pulitzer Prize A prestigious American award for outstanding achievement in newspaper, magazine, and online journalism, as well as for literature and musical composition.

surveillance Constant, close watch of a person, place, or method of communication.

telecommunications The transmission of information such as words, sounds, or images in the form of electromagnetic signals, as used by the internet, telephone, radio, or television.

whistleblower A person who reveals information about illegal or improper conduct to those in charge or to the public.

WikiLeaks An independent, nonprofit website designed to help people publish secret documents while remaining anonymous.

Books

Gellman, Barton. *Dark Mirror: Edward Snowden and the American Surveillance State*. New York: Penguin Random House, 2016.

Greenwald, Glenn. *No Place to Hide: Edward Snowden, the NSA, and the US Surveillance State*. New York: Metropolitan Books, 2014.

Harding, Luke. *The Snowden Files: The Inside Story of the World's Most Wanted Man*. New York: Vintage Books, 2014.

Websites

The Central Intelligence Agency

https://www.cia.gov/index.html

The official website of the CIA delivers stories about former employees, information on tours, and links to other recruiting materials.

The *Guardian*: The NSA Files

https://www.theguardian.com/us-news/the-nsa-files

The Guardian archives all of its stories relating to the NSA files received from Edward Snowden on this page.

The International Spy Museum

https://www.spymuseum.org

The mission of the International Spy Museum is to educate the public about espionage in an engaging manner and to provide a dynamic context that fosters understanding of its important role in, and impact on, current and historic events.

The National Security Agency/Central Security Service

https://www.nsa.gov

The official website of the NSA provides news stories, videos, images, and links to other digital information about the agency's activities.

We The People

https://petitions.whitehouse.gov

An official government website where the public can prepare a petition for the White House about an issue that matters to them, then circulate it for signatures of support. If the petition attracts one hundred thousand signatures within thirty days, the petition is submitted and is guaranteed a response from the government.

Videos

Citizenfour

https://citizenfourfilm.com

This 2014 documentary by Laura Poitras covers the spying scandal touched off by Edward Snowden's unauthorized release of NSA secrets.

NSA Spying: Has the Government Lost an Important Tool

http://www.cnn.com/videos/tv/2015/06/01/nsa-spying-powers-gellman-lead-intv.cnn

Pulitzer Prize–winning reporter Barton Gellman discusses the ramifications of Edward Snowden's revelations with CNN.

NSA Spying on Allies is Not On

https://www.theguardian.com/world/2013/oct/24/angela-merkel-nsa-spying-allies-not-on

German president Angela Merkel expresses her disappointment over the NSA's monitoring of her phone and collection of other information about allies in a video posted by the *Guardian.*

Books

D'Orazio, Valerie. *Beyond: Edward Snowden*. Marblehead, MA: Bluewater Productions, Inc., 2014.

Fidler, David P. "US Foreign Policy and the Snowden Leaks." In *The Snowden Reader*, edited by David P. Fidler, 52–69. Bloomington, IN: Indiana University Press, 2015.

Gardner, Lloyd C. *The War On Leakers: National Security and American Democracy, from Eugene V. Debs to Edward Snowden*. New York: The New Press, 2016.

Rall, Ted. *Snowden*. New York: Seven Stories Press, 2015.

Scheuerman, William E. "Taking Snowden Seriously: Civil Disobedience for an Age of Total Surveillance." In *The Snowden Reader*, edited by David P. Fidler, 70–90. Bloomington, IN: Indiana University Press, 2015.

Schwarz, Frederick A. O., Jr. *Democracy in the Dark: The Seduction of Government Secrecy*. New York: The New Press, 2015.

Magazines

Aleksander, Irene. "The Snowden Plot." *New York Times Magazine*, September 4, 2016.

Online Articles

Biography.com Editors. "Daniel Ellsberg Biography." Biography.com, April 2, 2014. http://www.biography.com/people/daniel-ellsberg-17176398.

Cole, Matthew. "Snowden: Feinstein a Hypocrite for Blasting CIA Spying." NBC News, March 11, 2014. http://www.nbcnews.com/storyline/cia-senate-snooping/snowden-feinstein-hypocrite-blasting-cia-spying-n49881.

Editorial Board. "The Post's View: No Pardon for Edward Snowden." *Washington Post*, September 17, 2016. https://www.washingtonpost.com/opinions/edward-snowden-doesnt-deserve-a-pardon/2016/09/17/ec04d448-7c2e-11e6-ac8e-cf8e0dd91dc7_story.html.

Gass, Nick. "White House: Snowden 'Is Not a Whistleblower.'" *Politico*, September 14, 2016. http://www.politico.com/story/2016/09/edward-snowden-not-whistleblower-earnest-228163.

Gladwell, Malcolm. "Daniel Ellsberg, Edward Snowden, and the Modern Whistle-blower." *New Yorker*, December 19 and 26, 2016. http://www.newyorker.com/magazine/2016/12/19/daniel-ellsberg-edward-snowden-and-the-modern-whistle-blower.

Greenwald, Glenn. "WashPost Makes History: First Paper to Call for Prosecution of Its Own Source (After Accepting Pulitzer)." *Intercept*, September 18, 2016. https://theintercept.com/2016/09/18/washpost-makes-history-first-paper-to-call-for-prosecution-of-its-own-source-after-accepting-pulitzer.

Harwood, William H. "Whistleblower or Traitor, Snowden Must Shut Up." *Huffington Post*, January 23, 2014. http://www.huffingtonpost.com/william-h-harwood/whistleblower-or-traitor-_b_4143834.html.

Herb, Jeremy, and Justin Sink. "Sen. Feinstein Calls Snowden's NSA Leaks and 'Act of Treason.'" *Hill*, June 10, 2013. http://thehill.com/policy/defense/304573-sen-feinstein-snowdens-leaks-are-treason.

Ingram, Mathew. "Here's Why the Washington Post Is Wrong About Edward Snowden."*Fortune*, September 19, 2016. http://fortune.com/2016/09/19/washington-post-snowden.

Isikoff, Michael. "NSA Program Stopped No Terror Attacks, Says White House Panel Member." NBC News, December 20, 2013. http://www.nbcnews.com/news/other/nsa-program-stopped-no-terror-attacks-says-white-house-panel-f2D11783588.

Kaplan, Fred. "The Leaky Myths of *Snowden*." *Slate*, September 16, 2016. http://www.slate.com/articles/news_and_politics/war_stories/2016/09/what_snowden_gets_wrong_about_its_hero.html.

Kramer, Andrew E. "Russia Extends Edward Snowden's Asylum." *New York Times*, January 18, 2017. https://www.nytimes.com/2017/01/18/world/europe/edward-snowden-asylum-russia.html.

McFadden, Cynthia, and William Arkin. "Russia Considers Returning Snowden to 'Curry' Favor With Trump: Official." NBC News, February 11, 2017. http://www.nbcnews.com/news/us-news/russia-eyes-sending-snowden-u-s-gift-trump-official-n718921.

Nelson, Steven. "Senate Passes Freedom Act, Ending PATRIOT Act Provision Lapse." *US News and World Report*, June 2, 2015. http://www.usnews.com/news/articles/2015/06/02/senate-passes-freedom-act-ending-patriot-act-provision-lapse.

"Pardon Edward Snowden." We the People, June 9, 2013. https://petitions.whitehouse.gov/petition/pardon-edward-snowden.

Radack, Jesselyn. "Whistle-Blowers Deserve Protection, Not Prison." *New York Times*, December 18, 2013. http://www.nytimes.com/roomfordebate/2013/06/11/in-nsa-leak-case-a-whistle-blower-or-a-criminal/whistle-blowers-deserve-protection-not-prison.

Risen, James, and Eric Lichtblau. "Bush Lets US Spy on Callers Without Courts." *New York Times*, December 16, 2005. http://www.nytimes.com/2005/12/16/politics/bush-lets-us-spy-on-callers-without-courts.html.

Savage, Charlie. "Chelsea Manning to Be Released Early as Obama Commutes Sentence." *New York Times*, January 17, 2017. https://www.nytimes.com/2017/01/17/us/politics/obama-commutes-bulk-of-chelsea-mannings-sentence.html.

Sullivan, Margaret. "As a Source—and a Patriot—Edward Snowden Deserves a Presidential Pardon." *Washington Post*, September 20, 2016. https://www.washingtonpost.com/lifestyle/style/as-a-source--and-a-patriot--edward-snowden-deserves-a-presidential-pardon/2016/09/19/dcb3e3f6-7e9c-11e6-8d0c-fb6c00c90481_story.html.

Topaz, Jonathan. "Kerry: Snowden a 'Coward … Traitor.'"
Politico, May 28, 2014. http://www.politico.com/
story/2014/05/edward-snowden-coward-john-kerry-
msnbc-interview-nsa-107157.

Von Drehle, David. "FBI's No. 2 Was 'Deep Throat': Mark
Felt Ends 30-Year Mystery of the Post's Watergate
Source." *Washington Post*, June 1, 2005. https://www.
washingtonpost.com/politics/fbis-no-2-was-deep-
throat-mark-felt-ends-30-year-mystery-of-the-posts-
watergate-source/2012/06/04/gJQAwseRIV_story.
html?utm_term=.a4a30a68ffef.

Gerry Boehme is an author, editor, speaker, and business consultant who loves to travel and to learn about new things.

Gerry has written books for students dealing with many subjects, including famous people who have made a difference in other people's lives. He has also spoken at conferences around the world.

Gerry graduated from The Newhouse School at Syracuse University and lives on Long Island, New York, with his wife and two children.